The Knights of the Order of Saint-Lazarus

The Unsung Heroic Knights of the Crusades

Conrad Bauer

ISBN 9798357660404

Printed in the United States

Contents

The Leper Knights

We all know the story of the Crusades. How the pilgrims visiting holy sites were bullied by marauders, and Byzantine borders were harried by Islamic conquerors. These factors led a medieval pope named Urban to call all of Christendom to arms, in order to protect their Christian brethren in the East. But is there something we are missing here?

The very first Crusade was led by one Godfrey de Bouillon, and by all accounts, it was a spectacular success. After traveling thousands of miles, these Christian Crusaders swarmed down on Jerusalem and captured the city on July 14th, 1099. This event led to the creation of the so-called "Kingdom of Jerusalem."

As a result, Godfrey, who did not want to be a king— was officially dubbed "Defender of the Holy Sepulcher." Godfrey did not feel worthy of the title of "King of Jerusalem" but by dubbing him "Defender of the Holy Sepulcher" he was more or less declared to be pretty much the same thing.

Despite these semantics, this was just another means of signifying Godfrey's sovereignty over the realm, since the Christian holy site of the Church of the Holy Sepulcher, was under his direct control and protection. The Defender of the Holy Sepulcher was indeed the defender of the Kingdom of Jerusalem itself.

It was actually Bouillon's brother, Baldwin of Edessa, who would first be officially proclaimed "King of Jerusalem," receiving his crown on Christmas Day—December 25th, 1100. It was in defense of this fledgling crusader state that special monastic orders of knights—of which the Order of Saint Lazarus would ultimately form a part—were first created.

Most of the Christian knights had to go home after the main thrust of the Crusade was over. This meant that a skeleton crew of Crusaders would have to double down on their resources. So, what could not be achieved in numbers was secured through monastic discipline.

You can think of these monastic orders of knights such as the Templars, Hospitallers, and yes, the Order of Saint Lazarus, as being the Special Operations forces of the Middle Ages. Like a bunch of hardcore, medieval marines, you didn't need a large army when a handful of monastic knights could take out 100 men all on their own. These monastic orders lived and breathed combat and gave their life fully to the cause of defending the Holy Land.

As fearsome as these knights were, however, fighting was not all that they were capable of—and combat was not the only duty they maintained. For often enough, it was these battle-hardened warriors who also set up hospitals and cared for the sick and wounded. The very term "hospital" stems from that famed order of crusading knights, the "Hospitallers."

Just like the Hospitallers, the Order of Saint Lazarus set up quite a few field hospitals in the Holy Land. It's said that the first headquarters of what would become the "Knights of Saint Lazarus" however, was in a hospital for lepers that was already in existence. According to tradition, there was a leper hospital founded in the seaside city of Caesarea, by Saint Basil, all the way back in the late 4th Century.

Ever since the days of Christ, Caesarea had been a bustling hub of activity on the Mediterranean coast of the area known as the Levant. The hospital was founded when the Roman Empire still had hegemony over the region, prior to the Levant being conquered by the armies of Islam. But although the Romans (Byzantine Romans at least) lost the Holy Land, the conquering Islamic overlords were kind enough (and perhaps pragmatic enough) to leave the hospital entirely undisturbed.

It was probably realized that the hospital served a great purpose as it pertained to taking care of the sick—especially those with such a fearful illness as leprosy. So it was that this hospital community was left alone to continue its vital function. It was found entirely intact by the time of the First Crusade, which reclaimed Jerusalem and the surrounding regions in 1099. The Crusaders then duly reorganized the hospital, and it became known as the "Hospital of Saint Lazarus."

Just as the Christian stewardship of the Levant had been resurrected after being dead for over 400 years, the hospital was also revitalized as a new and important hub of Crusader activity. The hospital would become a very important weigh station for pilgrims, as well as those who chose to settle down in the region.

The Establishment
of the Order

"One of the most astonishing things that are talked of is that though the fires of discord burn between the two parties, Muslim and Christian, two armies of them may meet and dispose of themselves in battle array, and yet Christian and Muslim travelers will come and go between them without interference. The Christians impose a tax on the Muslims in their land which gives them full security; likewise, the Christian merchants pay a tax on their goods in Muslim lands. The soldiers engage themselves in war, while the people are at peace and the world goes to him who conquers. Such is the usage in the war of the people in these lands. The state of these countries in this regard is truly more astonishing than our story can convey. May God by his favor exalt the word of Islam."
-Ibn Jubayr

Research into the Order of Saint Lazarus can sometimes be frustrating due to certain gaps in the written historical record. For those who are in search of clear-cut portrayals of events in the lives of the Lazarites, digging up these precious details can prove to be an elusive task. Especially when compared to some of the more well-documented monastic orders of the period, such as the Hospitallers and the Templars.

There is even some suggestion that perhaps the Order of Saint Lazarus was initially just an offshoot of the Hospitallers, with the only real separation of the two orders occurring at some point in the 1120s, at the behest of one "Boyand Roger" who was subsequently made the master of the order.

In the midst of much obscurity, there is some verified documentation of the hospital dating back to at least 1128, which at least gives some mention of the landmarks near the facility. The document mentions "a dwelling for lepers located between the Tower of Tancred and Saint Stephen's Gate."

It's said that the leper hospital in Jerusalem could house up to 1000 people at any time and actually consisted of two "separate areas" which allowed for those who were contagious with leprosy to remain generally isolated from those who were not openly contagious with the disease. This did not mean that there was zero interaction between healthy and non-healthy residents, but eating and sleeping quarters between those who were infected and those who were not—remained quite separate.

This separate living situation was imposed by a rigid schedule as it pertained to eating and sleeping, as well as harsh punishments enforced if the regulations were ever broken. The rules of the hospital were enforced by a so-called "warden" who made sure that all procedures were followed.

There is also, another fragmentary document in existence, which describes how the then Crusader King Fulk, and his Queen Melisende, gifted an estate to the order which had belonged to a "Baldwin of Caesarea."

It was about a decade or so later, in 1135, that a certain "Baron Roger de Mowbray" just back from the Second Crusade actually handed over an entire manor in England to yet another chapter of the order. The fact that the Order of Saint Lazarus was now expanding all the way to Britain is a strong testament to how crucial the group was viewed.

The order's members were important not only as warriors—but also for their work in hospitals for lepers and those with similar conditions who might need such treatment. By 1146, even more, English land would be gifted when the Earl of Arundel ceded territory in Norfolk to this monastic order of lepers. In 1159, Queen Melisende also oversaw the implementation of a so-called "leper house" which would be used to house even more lepers who needed regular treatment.

Further indicative that leprosy was a major focus of the community, was the fact that it was around this period that a legal statute known as "Livre au Roi" was put in place, making it common practice for any Crusading knight who happened to contract leprosy, to be automatically placed within the ranks of the Order of Saint Lazarus. The law specifically stated that it was within the order of the Lazarites "where it is established that people with such an illness should be."

Even more interesting, further instructions provide what should happen to not only the knight who was stricken with leprosy but also the leprous knight's family and property. It's stated that should that knight have a wife, provisions should be made for her to "enter a convent." Any property would then go to the knight's children or "heirs."

If there were no heirs, however, then the property would revert back to "their Lord." In the feudal society of the day, this might have meant several things. It could be that a baron who had overriding authority could claim the property, or someone with even more clout might become a claimant.

Interestingly enough, it would be Baldwin of Caesarea's descendant—Baldwin IV (the so-called Leper King) who would later become a tremendous benefactor to the order. Yes, Baldwin himself had leprosy—a startling discovery made when he was just a young princeling. But he handled it well, and even though he was in terrible pain and covered with sores, he would never fail to lead his troops out into battle— the mere sight of his scarred visage striking terror in the hearts of the enemies of the crusaders.

It was Baldwin IV after all, who was able to send the forces of Saladin on their heels in 1177. The first documented historical mention of them as a unique monastic order of knights, in fact, dates back to the year 1112. The official title of the order is the "Fratres hospitalis Sancti Lazari Hierosolimitani" or as it would be translated, the "Hospitaller Brothers of Saint Lazarus of Jerusalem."

Although the word "Hospitaller" is in their title, this order is not directly linked to the original Hospitaller Knights. As mentioned, these knights frequently took care of the sick and injured, but much more than that, they made it their specialty to tend to those who had leprosy. It was for this reason that the order was referred to as "Brothers of Saint Lazarus." It is believed that the name itself was in reference to the leper named Lazarus who was mentioned in the Bible.

In the biblical story, Lazarus was a poor beggar plagued with leprosy, who suffered terribly in life, but was given a great reward in heaven. Some have also suggested that perhaps the name was inspired by the *other Lazarus* mentioned in scripture—Lazarus of Bethany, whom Christ is said to have raised from the dead.

Lepers were typically considered hopeless cases doomed to death, but to carry the name of one who was literally raised from the dead would indeed serve as some inspiration in the face of repeated adversity.

Rather than shying away from a dreaded illness that most would not want to have *anything* to do with—this monastic order of knights embraced the most ostracized members of society. There is a historic mention of the order in a kind of travel guide of unknown authorship, which came into circulation around the year 1130.

This guide makes mention of a group of lepers who were living between the "Walls of Jerusalem and the Tower of Tancred [modern-day Jaffa Gate]. And the Gate of Saint Stephen [modern-day Damascus Gate]." The travel guide most likely was telling pilgrims to avoid the site, since there was such a tendency to literally keep lepers at arm's length.

Another interesting historic mention comes to us by way of a medieval map which appears to have arrived

9

on the scene sometime in the 1130s. This map indicates the location of the so-called "Ecclesie Sancti Lazari" which served as a sanctuary for lepers. At the inception of the order, the Ecclesie Sancti Lazari served as the main hub of activity.

Here, the first monkish knights of the order took on lepers and other sick individuals, attempting to nurse them back to health. As mentioned, the primary scope of the order's initial mission was tending to the sick. It wasn't until the 1150s that the knights took on more of a role as direct combatants in the continuing conflict in the Holy Land.

It was in 1155 that the knights were first mentioned by name. For it was this year that a receipt would later be uncovered bearing testament to donations being rendered to a group called "Chevaliers & Freres de Saint-Lazare de Jerusalem." Funds were being donated to the order by way of England's King Henry II.

Yes, in order to function, the monastic orders were always in need of charitable donations wherever they could find them, and King Henry II, a big supporter of the cause, was a frequent donor. Similar to other orders, the Knights of Saint Lazarus were run by a headmaster and had several levels of leadership, from knights to nurses. The order had a strong sense of brotherhood, and even the patients in the group were considered brothers and sisters of the order.

This sense of fraternity allowed even the leprous members of the community to take part in monastic life. It gave them a sense of belonging as well as some sense of contribution to the community that they were a part of. Even so, due to the issue of contamination and the protocols of the day, the lepers would remain completely isolated from the outside world. They were confined within the community set up by the Order of Saint Lazarus at all times. All the same, those whom the world rejected, the Leper Knights embraced wholeheartedly.

The Expansion of the Order

"There is nothing intrinsic linking any religion with any act of violence. The Crusades don't prove that Christianity was violent. The Inquisition doesn't prove that Christianity tortures people. But [only] that Christianity did [at one time] torture people."
-Salman Rushdie

During the first few decades of the order's existence, the Brothers of Saint Lazarus saw tremendous growth. With the help of steady charitable funds, they were able to set up shop not only in Jerusalem but also in other outposts of the Crusader-controlled Levant area, such as Tiberias, Nablus, Ascalon, Acre, and even Caesarea. The group was so useful in its treatment of lepers, that chapters even sprang up in mainland Europe.

Here, funds continued to pour in for those interested in at least financially supporting the mission of the order. In this way, the Order of Saint Lazarus would become the sole refuge for some of the most unwanted members of society. Even more stunning, some of the knightly class afflicted with leprosy joined the ranks and created what was indeed a special contingent of "leper knights."

These knights were naturally men of daring, and considering their dreaded illness (which could ultimately be terminal), they were men who cast all fear to the wind. Riding headlong at the enemy, with no concern for their own wellbeing, the leper knights would fiercely tear right through their opponents.

The enemy fighters, realizing they were being besieged by a bunch of lepers, would become even more fearful and intimidated. Upon seeing this contingent of disease-ravaged opponents, they realized that they not only risked getting struck down with the swords of the Leper Knights but also becoming infected and struck down with the illness they carried!

Or as Leper Knight chronicler Sharar described the phenomenon, "Knights with leprosy who continued to perform their basic fighting function, an order in which brothers with leprosy lived alongside brothers enjoying good health under the authority of a master, himself suffering from leprosy—all this had never been unheard of in Europe of the twelfth and thirteen centuries."

But perhaps even more interesting was the fact that entirely healthy men began to join the order, devoting their lives to both the care of lepers, as well as fighting side by side with lepers. It has sometimes been pointed out that the Latin Vulgate translation of certain scripture, which inserted the Latin term for leper—leprum—into a famous piece of biblical scripture, may have had a little something to do with this.

The verse comes from Isaiah 53:3 and is often pointed to by Christians as an example of an Old Testament prophecy about Jesus Christ. The verse in modern English translations typically reads, "He is despised and rejected of men; a man of sorrows and acquainted with grief; and we hid as it were our faces from him; he was despised, and we esteemed him not. Surely he hath borne our griefs and carried our sorrows: yet we did esteem him stricken, smitten of God and afflicted."

The Latin translation of this same verse then read, "Despectum et novissimum viorum, virum dolorum et scientem infirmitatem, et quasi absconditus vultus eius et despectus, unde nec reputavimus eum. Vere languores nostros ipse tulit et dolores nostros ipse portavit, et nos putavimus eum quasi leprum et percussum a Deo et humiliatum."

For those with discerning eyes, the keywords in this translation are "quasi leprum." For it was these two words that would encourage a veritable generation of crusading knights to throw in their lot with lepers. They came to view Christ himself as one who was identified with the suffering of a leper, and as such, they felt that if it was good for the Messiah, then it was good enough for them as well.

Contemporary chronicler Gerard of Nazareth wrote a rather interesting account of those who were tasked with taking care of lepers. In his discourse, he spoke of one man in particular, by the name of Alberic, who was said to have been a rather "colorful character who wore a rough goat-hair shirt." This guy apparently would hang out at the leprosarium located just outside of the city gates.

The man was a rough and tumble fellow, known— among other things—for yelling absurd "biting remarks" at people who passed by. Just imagine this guy standing around in goat-skin clothes, shouting at people that the end is near—and you probably get the picture. "There's no point in going to the Jerusalem

market and buying a bucket of lard! The end is near!"
Or so the goat-skin-clad man proclaimed.

But along with his "biting remarks" Alberic was also
known for his tender care and treatment of the lepers
under his charge. It's said that he regularly washed
the "ulcerous feet" of lepers, making sure that wounds
stayed clean and bandaged and didn't succumb to
infection. He also took it upon himself to carry those
who were already too sick to walk.

This sort of selfless service is certainly admirable and
is a trademark of the most dedicated of the order.
Alberic apparently also eschewed any material
comfort for himself, insisting on eating only the
leftovers of the lepers in his charge, and refusing to
cut his hair or take any other steps to secure his own
hygiene. It sounds a bit absurd to us today, but back
then, the notion of "penance" was a strong one, and
there were many who sincerely believed that the more
they deprived themselves, the better.

Again, it's perhaps a bit hard for us to understand
such things in today's world, but there were plenty of
cases of monks in monastic orders insisting on
sleeping upon wooden boards, or walking barefoot,
simply because they wanted to "crucify the flesh."
Today the most common form of penance, or self-
deprivation practiced in religious circles, is fasting.

Fasting is also a form of penance/self-deprivation
since you are temporarily depriving yourself of food,
while you reflect upon the divine. For most religious
believers today, fasting is probably the greatest extent
to which self-deprivation is experienced, and you are
unlikely to see any of the extremes of penitential

behavior that was practiced during the medieval period.

But yes, back in those days, there were indeed those, like good old Alberic, who sincerely believed that the more uncomfortable they made their own lives, the better off they were as it pertained to their faith. Even if someone like Alberic insisted on going without, such a thing wasn't really necessary from a practical standpoint, because the order itself was actually quite self-sufficient, as evidenced by the fact that they had their own mills and bakeries, as was well-documented by contemporary chroniclers of the period.

At the height of its influence, the Order of Saint Lazarus began to take on a distinctive presence. And as monastic orders tend to do, they developed their own coat of arms. The Order of Saint Lazarus would be known as the "Bearers of the Green Cross." Their flags would be distinctive: sporting a flag with a white background, with an eight-pointed, green cross as the centerpiece. This flag of the "Green Cross" was always sure to be hoisted in battle, as well as hung over all of the order's monastic properties.

Many have asked throughout the years, why the order chose the color green. There is a legend that the color stems from the leper king—Baldwin IV. Kind Baldwin IV allegedly had some sort of mystical vision, which included a green cross, and upon his awakening, actually woke up grasping that same cross in the palm of his hand. Besides this legend, it has also been suggested that the order was actually influenced by the fact that green is a color of preference in the Muslim world.

Muhammad is said to have liked the color green, and even today many of the flags of Muslim-majority countries all over the world are dominated by green. If this is the case, this must have been a bit of diplomacy mixed with subterfuge on the part of the Order of Saint Lazarus. If for example, a band of Muslim marauders saw the green cross leading a caravan of pilgrims, they just might have thought twice about attacking it—maybe being a bit unsure of the allegiance of the warriors escorting the pilgrims.

Seeing all of that greenery being hoisted into the air, one could imagine a band of brigands, wondering, "Are these Christian pilgrims to pillage, or prisoners of some elite Islamic guard?" Since they had no idea who they were dealing with, maybe they would just leave them alone. A further deterrent, of course, might have been the physical condition of the green-clad guardians. The knights of Saint Lazarus all had varying degrees of illness, and some might have looked worse for the wear than others.

These are all just theories and speculation about the order of course, and in reality, there could be nothing at all to them. Really, it could very well be that the founders of the order simply liked the color green. In addition to having green on their flags, the individual members also sported a black and white robe adorned with a green cross.

It was during the reign of the aforementioned King Baldwin IV, that the order really began to expand. Before Baldwin IV even ascended to the throne, his father Amalric, made sure that the charitable order was strong enough, perhaps sensing that his own son might one day have to make use of its services.

According to writer and historian Max Ellul, Baldwin IV's father was indeed a "special contributor to the Lazarite cause." In the later years of his reign, he was noted to have specifically donated a sum of 72 bezants to the order on a yearly basis. This was a large sum of money, which had been largely collected from the toll taxes paid by pilgrims passing through the Gate of David on their way to visit the holy sites.

The order put donations such as this to good use. They used them not only to care for the sick, but to finance their own mills, bakeries, and other self-sustaining industries. In 1150, there is even a receipt found recording the Order of Saint Lazarus' purchase of its own vineyard for the incredible sum of 1000 bezants. It was feats such as this that would ensure that the Order of Saint Lazarus would prosper for some time to come.

The Leper King and the Order of Saint Lazarus

"We are all humans and all deserve the same respect and attention."
-Lazarus of Bethany

The man who would one day become known as the "Leper King", Baldwin IV, began life in the year 1161. He was the son of Amalric, the former count of Jaffa, and his spouse Agnes of Courtenay. It was Amalric's older brother who had been King Baldwin III, and from whom the name Baldwin IV was derived. Amalric knew that his son was destined to one day be king— so much so that it's said that on the day of the boy's christening when he was asked what present he would give his son, he joked, "The Kingdom of Jerusalem."

Such remarks did indeed seem like a joke at the time they were made since at that time King Baldwin III was only in his 30s and firmly on the throne. He was also married to a young bride, capable of producing many heirs. So, the notion that something might happen to blot out Baldwin III's family line, forcing the kingship to go to Baldwin III's younger brother Amalric, and subsequently his son Baldwin IV, seemed preposterous.

Yet, just a couple of years after Amalric recklessly spoke those words with abandon, his brother Baldwin III abruptly perished without producing an heir. This meant that Amalric would indeed become king, and his son Baldwin IV would be the ultimate heir to the throne.

There was a problem from the very beginning, however, since the church decided not to recognize Amalric's marriage to his wife Agnes, on grounds that they were too closely related. It's rather absurd that these charges would be brought up six years and two children (the couple had produced both Baldwin and his sister Sibyl) after the fact. It's also interesting to note that the church authorities had such power over the lives of monarchs. This would most certainly not be the case in later years. Just think of England's bigamist monarch, King Henry the Eighth.

Amalric's marriage was officially rejected over claims that the couple was "related within the prohibited degrees." They were apparently related within the "fourth degree" to be exact since they shared a mutual ancestor in the form of one great, great grandfather by the name of "Burchard of Monthlery." And incredibly enough, in order to stake his claim on the kingship, Amalric readily complied with Church wishes and had his marriage annulled.

The children were fortunately spared the humiliation of being made illegitimate, however, because, after an entreaty to the pope, they were given an official "exoneration." Nevertheless, all of this meant that little Baldwin IV would grow up barely even knowing his own mother. And when he himself would later be stricken with leprosy, it would only give the gossip of the Kingdom of Jerusalem even more ammunition.

Despite all of the drama, however, Amalric had attempted to make the best of the situation. He even went so far as to make a politically dynamic union with the powerhouse just north of the Crusader States—the Byzantine Empire—by marrying one of Byzantine Emperor Manuel's great nieces: Byzantine princess, Maria Comnena.

Baldwin IV would never get along too well with his new stepmother and their relationship would be described as rather "cool" at best. Baldwin himself was kept rather busy and wasn't in the house that often, likely sparing Jerusalem's first family from any further friction.

At the tender age of nine, in fact, young Baldwin IV was sent off to study under a famed deacon—William of Tyre, who was said to have been the "most learned" individual in all of Jerusalem. He would live several years under the deacon's roof, studying and being groomed for one day taking the title of King for himself. It was while he was staying with William of Tyre, that the dreaded illness of leprosy was first detected. It was William of Tyre himself, who made the observation. He wrote a lengthy entry about the incident, which gives us vivid details of how it transpired.

William wrote:

> "*While he was staying with me it happened that, as he was playing with some boys of noble birth who were with him and they were pinching each other on the arms and hands with their nails, as children often do when playing together, the others cried out when they were hurt, whereas he bore it all with great patience, like one who is used to pain,*

although his friends did not spare him in any way. When this happened several times, and I was told about it, I thought it was a consequence of his patient disposition, not of his insensitivity to pain, and calling him to me I began to ask him questions about it. And finally, I came to realize that half of his right arm and hand were dead so that he could not feel the pinching at all, or even feel if he was bitten. Then I began to feel uncertain in my mind recalling the words of the wise man who said 'It is a certainty that a limb which is without feeling is not conducive to health and that a sick man who does not feel himself to so incur great danger.' His father was told, and after the doctors had been consulted, careful attempts were made to help him with poultices, ointments, and even charms, but all in vain. For with the passage of time we came to understand more clearly that this marked the beginning of a more serious and totally incurable disease. It grieves me greatly to say this, but when he became an adolescent, he was seen to be suffering from leprosy to a dangerous degree."

Understandably alarmed at this news of his son's leprosy, King Amalric sought to move heaven and earth in order to find some sort of treatment for his son. In doing so, he actually consulted with local Arabic-speaking physicians, which was practically unheard of at the time. Among the best of these local doctors was a man by the name of Abu Sulayman Dawud. Doctor Dawud would play a long and powerful role in the boy-king's life as both healer and mentor.

Still, life was hard for one who was diagnosed with leprosy, and the specter of disease, pain, and isolation, presented a rather grim future. Interestingly enough, however, thanks to the Order of Saint Lazarus, the situation for lepers in the Kingdom of Jerusalem was much more hopeful than it might have otherwise been. The Order was in full use by then, as was noted by a contemporary of the times, who stated that some "700 men" lived within the walls of the leper hospital just "outside the city of Jerusalem."

It's now widely assumed that if Baldwin IV was diagnosed with leprosy while still a child—as William of Tyre's account suggests—he would have been made a member of the Order of Saint Lazarus by the time he "came of age." All of this was of great concern for Amalric, who began to seriously set his sights upon his daughter Sibyl as a more likely heir than his disease-ravaged son.

He began planning ahead, by seeking out politically advantageous marriages for his young daughter, should she one day become Queen. This was not meant to be, however, and Amalric perished before finding a suitable suitor for Sibyl. He died of a bad case of dysentery, in the year 1174, at just 38 years of age. This meant that plans would go forward for Baldwin IV—the Leper King—to ascend to the throne.

Despite some of the misgivings, it's said that the crowning was an elaborate sort of fanfare and one in which the orders—including the Order of Saint Lazarus—were likely in attendance. Baldwin was only 13 years old at the time, and would not be considered a fully-fledged king until he reached the age of 15. In the meantime, he would be stewarded by others close to the throne. Even though he was stricken with leprosy, the boy-king was apparently otherwise in good health. As was noted at the time by William of Tyre.

William stated:

> *"He made good progress in his studies and as time passed he grew up full of hope and developed his natural abilities. He was a good-looking child for his age and more skilled than men who were older than himself in controlling horses and in riding them at a gallop. He had an excellent memory and he loved listening to stories. He was inclined to be thrifty, but he always remembered the good things that people had done for him, and the bad things as well. He was very like his father; not only did they look alike, but they were of similar build. They walked in the same kind of way and their speech patterns were similar. He had a quick understanding, but he had a stammer. Like his father, he had a passion for hearing about history, and he paid attention to the good advice which he was given."*

Regardless of this glowing description, however, the life of a leper was still quite difficult. And it certainly didn't help matters that the Third Lateran Council of 1179 had issued a special decree that "lepers should be identified and separated" as "the dead among the living." Normally a leper would be absolutely shunned—even those who fought and battled as leper knights would be cut off from society, spending the majority of their time in special facilities designed specifically for lepers.

Demonstrating the degree of this separation, lepers of the Order of Saint Lazarus even had their own special Mass. According to Saint Lazarus chronicler Max Ellul, the Mass given for lepers was "one of the most touching in the ecclesiastical liturgy." As Mr. Ellul describes it, "The cleric, after celebrating Mass for the infirm, put on a surplice and a stole, gave holy water to the leper, and then led him to the lazar-house of the Order."

They were not led to the general proceedings, you see, but to an entirely separate facility, to observe an entirely separate ceremony. And the words are indeed both tragically sad, as well as strangely heartwarming. Looking directly into the eyes of the afflicted, the priest spoke the following words:

> *"My brother, poor dear child of the good God, by suffering much sadness, tribulation, sickness, and other adversities of this world, one comes to the kingdom of Paradise, where there is no sickness, no adversity, but all are pure and clean, without spot or stain, brighter than the sun, whither you shall go, please God; but on condition that you be a good Christian and bear this trial patiently. May God give you the grace to do so. For, my brother, such separation as this is only corporal: as to the spirit, you always remain as free as ever you were, and will have a share in all the prayers of our holy Mother the Church as if you were daily present at the divine service along with the others. And as for your little wants, good*

people will provide for them, and God will not
forsake you. Only take care to have patience:
God is with you. Amen."

These were meant to be words of encouragement, and perhaps a much-needed softening in preparation for the tremendous blow to come. Next, the priest would instruct the leper how they are to conduct themselves, going into great detail on how they are to separate themselves from the general population at all costs.
Or as the priest solemnly decreed:

> *"I forbid thee to ever enter a church, or a*
> *monastery, or a market, or a mill, or a*
> *procession, or the company of the people. I*
> *forbid thee to appear out of thy house without*
> *thy lazar-dress so that thou mayest be known,*
> *or to appear barefooted. I forbid thee ever to*
> *wash the hands or anything that thou wearest*
> *at a bank or a fountain, or to drink there; and if*
> *thou wishes to drink some water draw it in thy*
> *own barrel or thy own porringer. I forbid thee to*
> *touch anything that thou sellest, or that thou*
> *buyest until it is thy own. I forbid thee to enter*
> *any inn. If thou desirest wine, either by buying*
> *it or having it given thee, let it be poured into*
> *thy own barrel. (owning your own vineyard to*
> *make your own wine would indeed be useful in*
> *this case!) I forbid thee to dwell with any other*
> *woman than thy wife. I forbid thee if thou*
> *walkest along the roads and meet any person*
> *that speaks with thee, to answer before thou*
> *hast placed thyself away from that side whence*
> *the wind is blowing. I forbid thee to walk by any*
> *narrow lane, so that, if thou shouldest*

anywhere meet a person, he may not be the worse thereof. I forbid thee, if thou goest through any passage, to touch a well or the rope unless thou hast put on thy gloves. I forbid thee to touch children or to give them anything. I forbid thee to eat or drink from any other vessels than thy own. I forbid thee to eat or drink with any other persons than those of thy own sort." It was after all of these restrictions were stated, that the priest once again turned on compassion. He placed the clay on the leper's heads, and enjoined them to, "Die to the world: by born again to God! Oh, Jesus my Redeemer, thou hast formed me of clay; thou hast clothed me with a body: grant that I may return to life on the last day!"

All of this certainly serves to demonstrate just how foreboding and isolated the life of a leper really was. But since Baldwin IV was king, of course, he could hardly live a life of complete isolation. For him, special consideration had to be made. At the start of Baldwin's kingship, the Crusaders had a dominant grasp of much of Palestine, as well as Syria.

Nevertheless, there were many vulnerabilities along the eastern frontiers. There was also the difficulty of cohesion among the Crusader states—Jerusalem, Tripoli, and Antioch were all more or less working independently of each other—even though their militaries would indeed work closely together when necessary. There was also the matter of the Byzantine Empire.

As a consequence of the deceased Amalric's marriage to a Byzantine princess, he granted many concessions to the Byzantine Emperor. He was even the very first Crusader King to make an official state visit to the Byzantine capital of Constantinople. With Amalric succeeded by Baldwin IV, the question then remained of how much of these concessions would continue to be obliged.

Baldwin IV's mother Agnes, in the meantime, had managed to work her way back into her son's life. She was a virtual stranger to the young man, but with a little effort, and thanks to Baldwin's willingness to accept her support, they managed to become reacquainted with each other. According to Max Ellul, Baldwin grew quite fond of his mother and in his later years would very much depend on her care and comfort, as his physical health deteriorated.

Others, however, were a little more than suspicious that his mother's "care and consideration" for her son, were merely part of a larger scheme to worm her way into the position of Queen, should her son perish prior to coming of age. This is of course a highly cynical view, and not all historians share it—but it is one interpretation of events all the same.

Nevertheless, Baldwin IV did indeed live to be a fully-fledged King in his own right, reaching the end of his regency on July 15th, 1176. His mother remained a strong influence on him, however, and it was in fulfillment of her request that he appointed one Joscelin of Courtenay as his prime minister. Despite what any naysayers may have thought about it at the time, this was a wise choice.

And it was Courtenay that prompted young King Baldwin IV to take a more proactive approach against the enemies of his kingdom. Ever since his father had perished and the Kingdom of Jerusalem had been in its perilous transition to Baldwin's reign, there had been many adversaries just itching to test the new leader.

Prior to this, the previous acting regent—Raymond III of Tripoli, had been basically practicing a disastrous policy of appeasement. And the previous year had agreed to a dubious "peace" agreement with the Muslim commander, Saladin. This peace ultimately freed Saladin—who had substantial holdings in Egypt—to conquer his Islamic opponents in Syria, beginning an encirclement of the Kingdom of Jerusalem that would prove to be its undoing.

Courtenay believed the best approach would be to take the fight to Jerusalem's enemies, rather than inevitably wait for their aggression to come home to roost. Baldwin agreed and refused to abide by the peace agreement that had been made with Saladin. It was this proactive policy that had Baldwin leading a punitive raid that same July, launching an expedition in Damascus, while the Sultan who ruled over the city was away in Aleppo.

The following year, in November of 1177, King Baldwin IV scored a great win for his kingdom. Despite his serious illness, the King was known to be both a skilled rider and a ferocious warrior. He proved as much when he led an army that managed to achieve such a spectacular victory against the forces of Saladin—the conquering Muslim commander was temporarily stopped in his tracks entirely.

As incredible as Baldwin IV the Leper King's leadership proved to be, everyone knew that his time on this Earth was going to be very limited. It was also known that he would never marry and therefore never produce a direct heir to the throne. It was for this reason, that pressure was applied to his sister Sibyl, to quickly beget an heir that could directly succeed Baldwin IV when it was necessary.

Although her husband William Longsword perished shortly after marrying her, during the short time of her marriage, Sibyl did indeed succeed in the task of producing an heir. She had become pregnant shortly before her husband's passing, and this pregnancy would produce a son she would name in honor of her leprosy-stricken brother—this child would come to be called: Baldwin V.

Saladin was on his heels in the meantime and was forced to enter into a truce with Baldwin. The truce was set to expire in 1182. Baldwin was not idle during this period and spent every waking moment mobilizing his forces and uniting his allies, in preparation for the inevitable renewal of conflict once the truce expired. Thanks to these tireless efforts, when Saladin predictably renewed his campaign against the Crusaders in 1182, they were ready for it, and their ferocious response was enough to make Saladin think twice.

Saladin ended up calling off the attack on Jerusalem and decided to assault weaker rivals in Iraq instead. The following year, however, Baldwin IV's health took a disastrous turn. His body becoming increasingly ravaged by leprosy, and he was no longer able to ride his horse into battle. As the disease progressed, even his vision failed him, and he became virtually blind.

Even so, Baldwin insisted on being carried into battle, and even in his weakened state, the Leper King served as a great inspiration for all of the knights that surrounded him—most especially those who hailed from the Order of Saint Lazarus. Even as he wasted away before their eyes, Baldwin IV, the Leper King, fought until his dying breath to ensure that the Kingdom of Jerusalem was not conquered under his reign.

And he succeeded in this task. Baldwin IV would perish in 1185, his leprous form entombed in the Holy Sepulcher of Jerusalem. It would be just two years later, in 1187, with the kingdom's leadership significantly weakened in the Leper King's absence, that the Crusaders would lose their hold on Jerusalem for good.

The Order of Saint Lazarus After the Fall of Jerusalem

"I warn you against shedding blood, indulging in it, and making a habit of it, for blood never sleeps"
-Saladin

As the Order of Saint Lazarus continued to expand, the situation in the Holy Land was destined to drastically change. For in the year 1187, the Crusader forces were soundly defeated in the Battle of Hattin. Here, the commander of the local Islamic forces— Salah al-Din (otherwise known as "Saladin")—proved himself as an ingenious and capable military general, tricking a large army of Crusaders into a trap, and then nearly annihilating them completely.

The Crusaders had previously avoided open battle and preferred to hole up in fortresses, only to unleash armies at times of their own discretion. This was indeed the most effective method for smaller, less robust fighting forces to use. But during the Battle of Hattin, they were lured out into the open and almost entirely vanquished. The results were completely disastrous for those who remained in Jerusalem.

With the main contingent of Crusaders snuffed out, Jerusalem was left entirely vulnerable, and soon Salah al-Din would come knocking on the very gates of the Holy City. Realizing that disaster was inevitable, the Order of Saint Lazarus mobilized their lepers and relocated them to the edge of Jerusalem where they might seek refuge and be safe.

The city ultimately withstood a 12-day siege before capitulating. All surviving Crusaders—including the Order of Saint Lazarus—were thereafter forced to relocate. To the great credit of the conquering Islamic commander Saladin, great mercy was shown to those who were defeated. Saladin especially permitted those who were deemed to be poverty-stricken (which most of those under the care of Saint Lazarus most certainly were), to leave without paying any kind of gratuity. No bribe would be required.

A checkpoint was actually set up right by the "House of Lazarus" in Jerusalem. Initially, at least, all were allowed to leave unmolested. But then an incident occurred that aroused the suspicions of one of Saladin's guards. The guard happened to notice one of the "poverty-stricken" individuals passing through the checkpoint carrying a large "gourd."

The curious sentry apparently got the idea that this person was trying to smuggle something outside through the city gates, by hiding it in this piece of large fruit. The sentry's suspicions were right. Upon further inspection, it was found that the gourd contained a stash of valuables. Despite claims to the contrary, the contents of this hollowed-out fruit indicated that this particular refugee was most certainly not poor. And from then on, those who left through the gate near the House of Saint Lazarus, would not be able to pass so easily.

It was the unmitigated disaster of this loss of Jerusalem that led to the launching of the Third Crusade, which managed to recapture much of the surrounding territories but fell short of retaking

Jerusalem. Interestingly enough, although Jerusalem was lost, and would not be regained by Christian Crusaders, one Crusader King—Baldwin IV—would remain as a sentinel in his tomb, as if he were standing watch from beyond the grave.

All of the other graves would be long desecrated, but Baldwin's tomb would remain undisturbed. This was due to a variety of reasons. For one thing, it was well known that Baldwin had leprosy and it was taboo to be near lepers—*even dead lepers.* Also, on top of all of this, Baldwin was remembered as a fairly noble figure even among his opponents. It could be said that there was also a superstitious fear that surrounded this larger-than-life figure. The tomb of Baldwin IV, the Leper King, would ultimately remain entirely undisturbed until a terrible fire broke out in 1808.

But as it pertains to the Order of Saint Lazarus, they would base themselves in surrounding localities, such as the far more fortified and better-defensible city of Acre. It was the stronghold of Acre which would become a major hub for not only the Knights of Lazarus, but also for the other major orders such as the Templars, Hospitallers, and the Teutonic Knights.

Upon relocating to the Crusader stronghold of Acre, the Knights of Saint Lazarus would be guaranteed a location to create a new Lazarus house, similar to the one they had in Jerusalem, just outside of the walls of Acre. This monastery/hospital/fortress would become known as the "Church of Saint Lazarus des Chevaliers."

Once they were settled in Acre, the Leper Knights were given generous financial contributions courtesy of one Humphrey de Toron and Walter Brisbane. These monetary donations were further enhanced by the year 1240 by way of the Order renting out a portion of the Montmusard region, as well as the granting of control over the so-called Tower of Lazarus.

Nevertheless, the order typically had more money going out than money coming in. Even with the help of generous benefactors, the cost of treating the sick as well as financing endless fighting in the Holy Land took its toll. Arrows alone cost a fortune. It's said that back in those days, for any prolonged time of siege warfare in which archers would be needed to man walls and towers, the defenders would require around 90,000 arrows just to keep up an adequate defense.

Often enough during defensive operations, however, the arrows would in fact run out, and the defenders would have to resort to throwing stones, garbage— and perhaps even corpses at their enemies. These missiles would most likely have the effect of annoying their enemies, rather than actually defeating them.

In order for the fighting force to stay effective, they had to be supplied and outfitted with the best armaments, and, of course, these armaments all cost money. Nevertheless, the order was known to be a disciplined one. And it's said that they were well drilled and maintained. In particular, the leper knights were good at maintaining cohesion on the battlefield.

They had a knack for highly orchestrated charges, and in particular were known for their great talent of suddenly wheeling around as one solid unit, sending their full force and fury straight into the enemy. One can only imagine the look of shock and fear from their opponents, to have the "living dead" Leper Knights suddenly tearing into the enemy front lines.

A third Crusade would be launched in 1188 in the meantime, in an attempt to recover Jerusalem. This Crusade was led by the dynamic figures of Richard of Lionheart of England, King Philippe Augustus of France, and the German potentate—Frederick Barbarossa. This Crusade had much promise but faced an early setback when Barbarossa accidentally perished by drowning, en route to the Holy Land.

Lionheart was able to seize much of the initiative, however, and led a formidable assault upon Saladin's forces in the Levant region. Although the ultimate prize of Jerusalem eluded him, Lionheart and his allies (including the Order of Saint Lazarus) were able to retake much of the surrounding territory that had been lost. Saladin himself would perish just a few years later in 1193, but regardless, Jerusalem would remain just out of the Crusader's reach.

As fearsome as the Order of Saint Lazarus was in battle, not all engagements turned out so well for the leper knights, and one of the most infamous of debacles faced by the order took place during the Battle of Gaza which was waged against the "Khwarazmians" in October of 1244. The Order of Saint Lazarus was also on the frontlines during the ill-fated Seventh Crusade which was commanded by France's King Louis IX.

Lasting roughly two years, from 1248 to 1250, King Louis IX made the disastrous decision to launch a Crusade with the aim of liberating the Holy Land, not by landing in the Levant area, but by stepping foot in Egypt. King Louis apparently thought that it would be a prudent strategy to gain ground in Egypt and then march northeast into (what he hoped) would be the soft underbelly of the Levant.

But there were several factors that the King and his Crusaders did not take into consideration and this particular crusade came to naught. All of this spelled disaster for the Knights of Saint Lazarus who participated in this exchange, and were basically annihilated by the man. The Knights of Saint Lazarus again saw action in 1253, this time in Ramleh, but met an even more inglorious end than they had suffered during the Crusade in Egypt.

This time, the Grandmaster of the order led a punitive raid on some local cattle, only to be surrounded by the enemy and killed nearly to the man. Or as chronicler Joinville detailed, "While the king was before Jaffa, the master of Saint Lazarus had spied out near Ramleh, a town some three good leagues away, a number of cattle and various other things which he thought to collect some valuable booty. So being a man of no standing in the army, and who therefore did exactly as he pleased, he went off to that place without saying a word to the king. But after he had collected his spoils, the Saracens attacked him, and so thoroughly defeated him that of all the men he had in his company no more than four escaped."

This account seems to indicate that the Leper Knights were going a bit rogue in this engagement and were under no direct orders from anyone else when they engaged in this doomed punitive expedition. It's also been suggested that the Leper Knights, due to their condition, may have been purposefully kept at arm's length. They were perhaps kept to the periphery, often inspiring them to go on scouting raiding missions away from the main encampment of Crusaders.

At any rate, back in Ramleh, the fighting did not go so well for the Lazarites and they were only saved from complete annihilation by way of King Louis IX. And upon the French King's departure from Acre in the year 1254, he actually took 12 Leper Knights with him to France. These members of the Order of Saint Lazarus he then tasked with setting up leper hospitals in France itself.

We find historical mention of the Knights of Saint Lazarus come up once again in 1255 when Pope Alexander IV made a specific note of the order. The Pope wrote of "a convent of nobles, of active knights and others both healthy and leprous, for the purpose of driving out the enemies of the Christian name." The Pope obviously considered the Leper Knights an active force in the religious warfare between the forces of Islam and the forces of medieval Christendom.

During this period, the Order of Saint Lazarus was also actively involved with the Knights Templar. The two orders aided each other both militarily as well as financially. In a show of goodwill, the Templars even granted the Leper Knights full use of their water reserves. This was very important since one stricken with leprosy had to follow restrictive prohibitions in regard to water consumption, making the gathering of an already precious resource in the often scorching desert environment of the Mideast, even more precious.

This kind gesture ended up paying the Templars back in 1258 when Acre was caught up in what has been described as a most tumultuous "civil disturbance." The incident involved a riotous outbreak of violence between armed factions of visiting Venetians, Pisans, and Genoese knights. The fighting was so bad that the Grandmaster of the Templars found himself caught in the crossfire between the armed camps.

It was the nearby Tower of Saint Lazarus just outside the walls of Acre, that provided the beleaguered Grandmaster of the Templars refuge. From here on, the Templars would indeed continue to serve as benefactors for their brother's order of Leper Knights. The two orders would remain close all the way up until the Templar's own dissolution as a knightly fraternity in 1312.

Along with the aid from their Templar brothers, the Order of Saint Lazarus the meantime was still dependent upon a wide range of charitable contributions and indulgences sent from abroad. It was Pope Urban IV, in 1261 who made the order officially under the dominion of the "Latin Patriarch of Jerusalem." These measures were then furthered by Pope Clement IV in 1265, who put all "houses of leprosy" in Europe under the direct control of the order.

As these institutional changes were being made, in the meantime the Crusaders of the Holy Land were facing repeated reverses. The denizens of what remained of the Crusader states found themselves barely hanging on. And often enough, they were practically clutching at straws just to fend off one incursion after another. As the 13th Century drew to a close, there was a brief glimmer of hope from an unexpected source when Mongol armies began to decimate nearby Islamic strongholds.

The Mongols provided a strange opportunity for the Christian Crusaders since they were—for the most part—neither of the Islamic faith nor Christian believers. The Mongols despite their reputation for brutality, were actually extremely tolerant of religions. They typically couldn't care less what religion was practiced by the people they conquered, as long as they abided by Mongol rule. And under Mongolian hegemony already were vast swaths of Christians and Muslims alike.

As the Mongols continued to antagonize the Muslim world, however, they began to take a sharper stance against the Islamic polities of the region. This antagonism would break out into direct conflict, and the Crusaders sought to make themselves the direct beneficiaries of it. And so it was in 1281, that a contingent of knights from the Order of Saint Lazarus actually teamed up with Mongols in an offensive in Marqab, Syria. But these brief glimmers of hope were rather quickly dashed.

Eventually, this would lead up to the most stunning defeat of all—the loss of Acre in 1291. With the loss of Acre, the last and final toehold in the Holy Land was lost for good. The siege was led by Islamic warlord, Sultan Al-Ashraf, who took on the Templar Knights who were tasked with defending Acre. Alongside this last stronghold of Templar Knights, some 25 Knights of Saint Lazarus were holed up.

These knights may have been small in number, but they fought with all they had in them. The leader of the opposition forces—Sultan al-Ashraf—launched his assault in March of 1291. At that time, Acre was full of those seeking refuge from the coming storm, and the civilian population of the city was close to 40,000 people.

Al-Ashraf camped his forces around the besieged city and ordered the first direct attack to commence on April 5th. As was typically the tradition during Muslim conquest, Al-Ashraf gave the defenders the opportunity to capitulate. The Sultan promised to spare their lives as long as they agreed to abide by certain conditions—and most importantly *to submit to Islam.* The term "Islam" itself means "submission."

And all throughout the Muslim conquests of history, this submission typically meant that Islam would become the dominant religion of conquered regions. Civilians who were "people of the book" that is— believers in monotheism such as those who adhered to Judaism and Christianity—were usually permitted to keep their religion, but would be forced to pay a special tax called the "jizya" and would quite literally be treated as second-class citizens, set apart from their Muslim rulers.

It's worth noting that as bad as all this might seem from a modern perspective, it was typically more generous than what many conquering Christians might have allowed. Nevertheless, for these Christian Crusaders, the conditions presented were not anything that they could ever possibly agree with. Before the gates of the city, the Sultan declared the following:

"The Sultan of Sultans, King of Kings, Lord of Lords, al-Malik al-Ashra, the Powerful, the Dreadful, the Scourge of Rebels, Hunter of Franks and Tartars and Armenians, Snatcher of Castles from the Hands of Miscreants, Lord of the Two Seas, Guardian of the Two Pilgrim Sites. We send you advance notice of our intentions and give you to understanding that we are coming on your part to right the wrongs that have been done. We do not want the community 0f Acre to send us any letters or gifts for we will by no means receive them."

These words were meant to indicate that the time for bartering and negotiation was over. There were only two choices: surrender or die. For the Crusading knights that defended Acre, the choice was easy. They would give their lives to protect the city and those under their charge. But this wasn't just a desperate, mindless last stand. Those in charge of the city did indeed have a coherent strategy to work with. And if every single aspect of that said strategy fell into place and worked without a hitch, it was possible (however unlikely) that they could have fended off this attack.

The Crusaders were greatly outnumbered by their opponents, but it's much easier to defend a city than to take one. The two key factors on which ultimate success would rely would be both defending the city's fortifications, as well as destroying the enemy's siege engine. The medieval siege engines are the various pieces of apparatus used to scale walls, blow holes in perimeters, or otherwise destroy the protective barriers around a city.

It was on April 15th, that a group of Leper Knights worked to achieve the latter. They exited through the Gate of Saint Lazarus under the cover of darkness, and under the aegis of the master of their order—William de Beaujeu—they sought to seek out the enemy's siege engines and render them inoperable. This was just the kind of special operations action that the stealthy and fearless Order of Saint Lazarus was made for. And the results would have been a big win for Acre's defenders, if only it had worked as planned. But it didn't.

In the darkness, it was hard to maneuver, and the horses that the Leper Knights rode actually tripped over the ropes staked in the ground and attached to the tents of the enemy encampment. Tumbling head over heels, these knights were easy prey for the alerted sentries of the Sultan. After this miserable failure, hopes were dashed. It was roughly a month later on May 14th, that the Sultan ordered the main assault on Acre. The city walls were demolished, and the enemy came pouring in.

The Crusading Knights, with some of the Order of Saint Lazarus among them, fell back to the fortified Templar House where they made a desperate last stand. Even when it was clear that defeat was near, the knights fought so ferociously that the Sultan attempted negation. It was promised that the civilians would be unharmed if the knights put down their weapons. Reluctantly, the knights agreed.

But as soon as enemy soldiers came into the Templar house where several women and children were holed up, the enemy troops began to mistreat the frightened civilians. Disgusted, the knights immediately picked up their swords and hurled themselves at the abrasive intruders. They fought so ferociously they pushed them back out into the courtyard.

The Sultan, himself quite weary of all the drama, was fed up at this point, and ordered explosives to be put around the building to blow a hole into it. The explosives turned out to be too powerful, however and managed to severely damage the very foundations of the Templar house.

What happened next must have truly been a scene of Biblical proportions. It was the Old Testament hero Samson after all, who when surrounded by enemies famously asked God for "one more chance" to vanquish his foes. Although blinded and chained to a stone column in the enemy temple, it's said that God granted Samson the strength to push over the stone columns he was chained to, thereby causing the whole roof of the structure to collapse, killing all who were inside.

Likewise, one could see a parallel to this, with what ultimately befell the Templar house where so many brave Templar Knights, as well as Leper Knights, were holed up. The Templars and Leper Knights too would have their last chance at vengeance. Similar to that biblical scene of Samson, the roof of the Templar

House collapsed just as the enemy forces were pouring in. Everyone inside was crushed to death.

The Crusading knights had lost their lives, but they did not lose their dignity and they saw to it that those under their charge were protected from vile harassment, even if they had to exit this life in order to do so. This would be the last dramatic chapter of the Order of Saint Lazarus in Acre.

The Exodus and Subsequent Diaspora of the Leper Knights

"The smell of gunpowder is sweeter to me than all the perfumes of Arabia."
-Pope Julius II

Acre fell on May 14th, 1291. The conquerors, this time around, were insistent on removing all traces of the Leper Knights. Even though when the armies of Muhamad first took the Holy Land from the Christian Byzantines in 637 AD, the Leper Hospital was allowed to survive and prosper; this time around it was demolished. As if wishing to quickly get rid of any memory of the Leper Knights, a mosque was erected over the wreck and ruin of what had been the Hospital of Saint Lazarus.

After this stunning blow, many surviving knights sought to create a new stronghold in the nearby Mediterranean island of Cyprus, and there were Knights of Saint Lazarus among their number. But without a local leper colony, the Order of Saint Lazarus had lost much of its purpose. As such, there were soon calls to have a local center for leprosy built right there on the island. Thanks to generous contributions from one "Bernard Fayssa of Narbonne" this intention was fulfilled in 1310. This site ultimately was transformed into an abbey called "Our Lady of Tyre."

49

Besides Cyprus however, it was actually in France that a large estate had been set aside for the Leper Knights, in the fief of Boigny, near the city of Orleans, which would become the main headquarters of the monastic order. It was with the end of defending the Holy Land, that many of the new monastic orders lost their primary reason for existence. Even though many of the orders, such as the Hospitallers and the Order of Saint Lazarus did just as much good on a humanitarian basis as they did in battle—their drain on resources became increasingly undesirable.

And as it pertained to the Knights Templar—once the mightiest of all the monastic orders—this perceived undesirability had fatal consequences. The French King, growing weary of having a virtual nation-state of knights encamped on his territory, schemed up a way to get them all charged as heretics. As a result, the Templar Knights' lands and wealth were confiscated, the order was disbanded, and their leaders were burned at the stake.

Determined not to share the same fate, the other monastic orders, such as Saint Lazarus, struggled to change with the times—attempting to forge a new reason for their very existence. This meant that much of the order's work would center around its humanitarian efforts, rather than its military prowess. The Order of Saint Lazarus itself had several land holdings and many of these properties were still being used to treat those who were afflicted with the scourge of leprosy. This was most especially the case after they were officially sanctioned for this task by Pope Clement IV.

By the early 1300s, the group was in command of a vast number of these treatment centers. Nevertheless, there was trouble brewing, since envious rulers sought to either expel the knights or tax them out of existence. Such things led to numerous legal battles between the knights and local rulers. The order could only breathe a sigh of relief when King Philippe IV of France officially reconfirmed the order in the year 1317.

Further crystalizing this ruling was the ecclesiastical order leveled by Pope John XXII in the following year of 1318, which tied the order directly to the Pope. This would mark the beginning of the order's long and slow decline. There were some bright spots, however, such as the establishment of a strong branch of the order in Scotland in 1308. This was done at the behest of the English master of the order—Burton Lazars.

Lazars signed a contract that gave control of the Scottish chapter of the order to a chaplain by the name of Roger de Robeby. The contract actually stated that Robeby would have control of the order indefinitely. Or as the exact words of the contract directly stipulated, Roger de Robeby would have control over the "houses in the border of Northumberland and the Kingdom of Scotland up to the end of his life."

Another interesting chapter for the Order of Saint Lazarus had popped up in the meantime, on the Italian island of Sicily. It seems that some of these Leper Knights had benefited from the warm climate of the Mideast, and were looking for a similar environment elsewhere for new leper colonies. Sicily seemed to fit that bill.

It was an island, on which the Leper Knights could create an isolated headquarters, and benefit from good weather, year-round. Aiding them in the establishment of their new Sicilian base was none other than the then "Hohenstuafen" potentate of the island—Emperor Frederick II. This branch of the Order of Saint Lazarus made its base right in the midst of sunny Capua, and would ultimately become an entirely separate institution from the rest of the Knights of Saint Lazarus.

By the 1400s, the Order of Saint Lazarus—like every other order of monastic knights—was in great decline. Their main purpose of defending the Holy Land was long gone. The uniqueness of the order and its emphasis on caring for lepers, however, gave it a continued lifeline of support. More changes were underway, however, when in 1489, Pope Innocent VIII, gave the remnants of the Order's assets over to the "Order of Saint John" or as they are perhaps better known, the "Hospitaller Knights."

This enabled Saint John's Grandmaster to essentially have the permission to oversee all of the proceeds from properties and charitable organizations of the Leper Knights. This would greatly alter the course of the Order of Saint Lazarus from here on. From this point on, the order would also be increasingly centered around its leper colonies located in France.

But in 1490, when the Pope attempted to forcibly merge the two orders together, the Leper Knights were not at all happy about it. There was indeed precedence for such a thing since prior to this the Pope had authorized the merger of the Livonian

Brothers of the Sword, to merge with the Teutonic Knights. The mainline branch of the Knights of Saint Lazarus displayed vigorous resistance to this notion, however, and insisted that they remain a separate order, with their own unique headquarters situated in Boigny, France.

The Hospitallers in the meantime was probably not quite so thrilled at the notion of hooking up with a bunch of lepers, and the pushback was minimal. For the time being the Order of Saint Lazarus would remain intact as a separate order. In 1493 (one year after Columbus discovered the New World no less) the group managed to elect a dynamic and powerful new leader in the form of "Francois d'Amboise."

Grandmaster Amboise sought to maintain a sense of legitimacy for the order. These efforts were then continued by his successor, Agnan de Mareul, who was made Grandmaster in the year 1500. As an interesting aside about Agnan de Maruel, he was a scion of the powerful Mareul family, which would do all it could to keep the leadership of the order in the family.

It was Agnan himself after all who would famously quit his position as Grandmaster in 1519, in order to recruit his 16-year-old nephew Claude Mareul—who would serve from 1519 to 1554—as the next Grandmaster of the Order of Saint Lazarus. Such a thing seems to be a pretty clear-cut case of nepotism in action. Nevertheless, the continued efforts of the Mareul dynasty to maintain the independence of the order were rewarded in 1505 when Pope Julius II issued an official Bull called "Romani Pontificis" which sought to do just that.

Even so, these official proclamations were not always fully recognized. And often enough seemed to fall flat. Much of this, was due to the changing times. Ever since the Reformation in the early 1500s, sparked by former Catholic monk—Martin Luther—many states in Europe were ceasing to listen to the Pope altogether.

Pope Pius V for example, made a great effort to reform the order in the 1560s, by making use of its charitable activities for lepers and expanding these good works to other leper hospitals. The efforts would only work, however, in regions that were still following the precepts of the Pope. In addition to this, leprosy in Europe was also in decline, rendering much of the services of the Lazarus houses entirely unnecessary.

Even more, changes were on their way in the meantime, when French King Charles IX made a proclamation, which entitled the "Duke of Savoy" to take control of properties in France that were previously under the jurisdiction of the Order of Saint Lazarus. The idea that some king could unilaterally seize the assets of an Order of Knights is distressing to contemplate. Especially considering what had already happened to the Templars, but this is indeed apparently what happened.

King Charles IX's successor Henry III, then flexed this royal muscle to an even greater degree, when in 1575, he actually ordered the then Grandmaster of the order—Francesco Salviati—to resign. Without much of a choice, Francesco Salviati did just that.

But Francesco proved himself to be a clever statesman in his own right. For, just as he was making his exit from the order, he "advised" the king that it would not be wise for him to give all of the order's properties over to the Duke of Savoy, should the duke decide to suddenly turn on him. The words of Francesco apparently made an impact, because the King of France suddenly reversed course, returned the seized estates, and even reinstated Salviati to the post of Grandmaster.

The fortunes of the Order—at least as it pertains to France—greatly improved from here. In 1664, many more lay hospitals were incorporated into being under the dominion of the Order of Saint Lazarus. This was then followed by the merger of many previous Hospitaller-owned holdings, into the Lazarus fold as well. This merger was completed in the year 1672.

Due to all of these lucrative acquisitions, the Order of Saint Lazarus once again became a financially solvent enterprise. It's said that in 1690 alone, the group raked in some 300,000 livres, which was an incredible sum back in those days. And within this amount, there were some individual commanderies/hospitals that averaged at least 1500 livres per year.

The Lazarite leadership who oversaw this windfall— Grandmaster Louvois—then had an even better idea. He saw that there was a growing interest in membership by way of the so-called "Knights of Grace." This was a special designation given to non-leper members of the order. These members typically were those who were seeking the distinction of gaining the status of a knight, without having to go through the typical hurdles of other military orders.

Grandmaster Louvois realized that new members would breathe new life into the order and greatly encouraged recruitment. As a result, the ranks of the Order of Saint Lazarus would swell to epic proportions. There was also a fee for membership known as the "passage fee." This was initially just 300 livres, but was subsequently raised to around 1000 livres. This too would ensure that the Order of Saint Lazarus would be on a good financial footing for some time.

The Order of Saint Lazarus, in the meantime, far from being a group of shunned lepers—was turning into an exclusive institution for the privileged. So much so in fact, that the French royal family even became involved with the membership. King Louis XVI was famously a member and had actually been appointed Grandmaster of the order itself when he was just a child. He would then hand the mastership over to his own brother—the future French King, Louis XVIII.

The order was now so entrenched with French royal power, most members probably assumed that they were on some rather rock-solid foundation. Little did they know however that a coming revolution would shake the very halls of French power and authority, and bring the Order of Saint Lazarus to its knees as a result.

The French Revolution was kickstarted by French ideologues who wished to create a more equal and just society. But as the proverb goes, sometimes it's the "best of intentions" that can "pave the way" to some rather disastrous results. And this was most certainly the case in the French Revolution.

The Revolution kicked off in 1789 after a mob of angry citizens, upset with a faltering economy and other social ills stormed an armed depot called the "Bastille." From here on out, armed mobs were able to seize control of much of the country. Then in the Fall of 1792, a National Convention of revolutionaries was held, which completely eradicated any notion of a French monarchy.

What was done on paper was then quickly followed up in real life, with the beheading of the King and Queen of France. That same year, the so-called Assembly of the Third Estate had issued a decree that all knightly military orders—including the Order of Saint Lazarus—be immediately abolished.

The French Revolution itself would then devolve into endless terror and bloodshed of the worst kind, as the knives of the revolutionaries turned against each other. In the midst of this tumult, a French General named Napoleon Bonaparte would seize power, ending the revolutionary fervor by inserting himself as dictator of Imperial France.

After leading much of the world into war, Napoleon was finally put out of action in 1815. Although later variations of the Order of Saint Lazarus have popped up, most historians consider the official Order of Saint Lazarus to have met its end during the tumult of the French Revolution, with no immediate resurrection forthcoming.

The Order of Saint Maurice

The previous chapter mentioned that most mainstream chroniclers consider the end of the Order of Saint Lazarus to have occurred during its abolishment during the French Revolution. But some contend that a variation of the Order did indeed live on, an Italian variation of the Leper Knights known as the "Order of Maurice."

This matter is still highly debated, but to understand it better, let's go ahead and dive right into the controversy. The history of the Order of Maurice can be traced back to February 13th, 1434, when one "Amadeo VIII of Savoy" instituted a branch claiming a connection to the Order of Saint Lazarus, which was dubbed the "Order of Saint Maurice."

The Order remained relatively obscure until a Papal Bull was issued in 1517, which seemed to legitimize some of the Order's claims. Around this time, an independent group of monastic knights claimed a connection to the Order of Saint Lazarus. In the Papal Bull of 1517, the pope gave the Grand Master of this Italian outfit authority over many leper hospitals in Italy and Sicily.

This organization once again came to attention in 1572, when its Grand Master, a Milanese noble by the name of "Gianotto Castiglione," incorporated most of the Commanderies in Italy under the charge of the Order of Maurice. The following year, in 1573, a special convention for the Order of Maurice was held near Nice, France. A contingent of the Order of Saint Lazarus was indeed in attendance, seemingly giving further legitimacy to the Order.

Trouble would come to this supposed chapter of Leper Knights during the French Revolution. However, when in 1796, after the French seized control of French territory and forced King Carlo Emanuele IV to flee to Sardinia. Many Knights of the Order of Maurice followed and set up shop on the island. The French imperialists seized the Order's assets under Napoleon Bonaparte on August 21st, 1800.

These, however, were returned once the Italian royal family returned to Italy. At the close of the Napoleonic wars, we find mention of the Order in "Royal Magistral" letters, issued on December 27th, 1816, which instituted some new regulations for the reinstatement of the Order. These orders were then updated once again by King Carlo Alberto on December 9th, 1831.

Among other things, the instructions spoke of new rewards for knights for their service and new uniforms. More updates to the Order occurred in 1851 in the meantime, when hereditary Commanderies were abolished, making sure that the Order of Maurice would be one of merit rather than one which espoused nepotism. The Italian King—Victor Emanuel II, is noted in this period for getting rid of much of the bureaucratic customs of the Order in further attempts to modernize it.

At any rate, the Order of Maurice would continue more or less undisturbed in this fashion until after the Second World War, when the Italian King Umberto II was deposed and sent into exile. Although technically not himself a fascist, Umberto was knee-deep in fascism, as his Prime Minister was none other than Benito Mussolini. The Italian people decided they had enough and thought they would get rid of both the king and the Order of Saint Maurice.

But little did they know, the king had other plans. Even in his exile, he claimed to have a "pontifically given right still" (remember that 1517 Papal Bull?) to nominate Grand Masters of the Order. And even from his perch in exile, he continued to do so as the official overseer of what was not an entirely charitable Order.

Even after the king's death, his son Prince Vittorio Emanuele sought to continue this tradition. Such things show that the Order of Maurice had some longevity, but it does not necessarily prove that the Order of Maurice is a direct descendant of the Order of Saint Lazarus.

In Consideration of the Selfless Service of the Leper Knights

The Leper Knights who hailed from the Order of Saint Lazarus are heroes of epic proportions. One could argue that they were even more heroic than the Hospitallers, or the Knights Templar since these brave men not only fought against armed opponents in combat but against the strife and stigma of their own illness. Life was certainly not easy for a leper in the Middle Ages. They were forced by the nature of their condition to live set apart from the rest of society.

Having said that, the interesting thing about the Leper Knights is the fact that they fought so hard for a society that ultimately rejected them. Just consider the Leper Knights holed up outside of the Gates of Jerusalem, or the Gates of Acre in the Holy Land. Out of fear of contagion, they were not allowed to mingle within the city walls. Yet, here these knights were perched as wardens on the outskirts of a city that would not normally allow them entry.

Yet if an adversary were to approach, it would be these socially rejected Leper Knights who would ring the alarm. And it was these knights who would give their lives out on the frontlines, making sure that the denizens of the city were protected. It is this kind of selfless service that goes above and beyond all human pretensions that makes this Order of Knights seem so noble and courageous.

63

Since the end of the official Order of Saint Lazarus, in the aftermath of the French Revolution, there have been several imitation orders have sprung up, no doubt inspired by the tremendous legacy that these knights have created. Even though these orders may not be considered official successors of the original order, they have adopted the ideals that the Order of Saint Lazarus espoused. Even if the official Order of Saint Lazarus has not been resurrected outright, its tremendous legacy most certainly lives on.

Made in United States
Orlando, FL
01 June 2023

33689520R00039